My Path to Math

123456789

MONEY

Penny Dowdy

Crabtree Publishing Company

www.crabtreebooks.com

Author: Penny Dowdy
Coordinating editor: Chester Fisher
Series editor: Jessica Cohn
Editors: Reagan Miller, Molly Aloian
Proofreader: Crystal Sikkens
Project coordinator: Robert Walker
Production coordinator: Margaret Amy Salter
Prepress technician: Margaret Amy Salter
Logo design: Samantha Crabtree
Project manager: Santosh Vasudevan (Q2AMEDIA)
Art direction: Rahul Dhiman (Q2AMEDIA)
Design: Tarang Saggar (Q2AMEDIA)
Photo research: Anju Pathak (Q2AMEDIA)

Photographs:
Bigstockphoto: Stajduhar: p. 14 (left)
Corbis: Gabe Palmer: p. 11
Dreamstime: Cammeraydave: p. 14 (right); Dndavis: p. 16; Klikk: p. 17
Getty Images: Dave King/Dorling Kindersley: p. 21 (mixed coins-top)
Istockphoto: Nina Shannon: p. 21 (girl); Mike Sonnenberg: cover; Baileyworld: p. 10
Jupiterimages: Dave & Les Jacobs: p. 18; Radius Images: p. 20; Zedcor Wholly Owned: p. 9
Photographersdirect: Michael Robin Photography (onlinegallery.com): p. 7
Shutterstock: Mario Bruno: p. 8 (left), 15 (top); Kenneth Cheung: p. 21 (Canadian bill); Elnur: p. 21 (stacks of coins and American bills); EuToch: p. 15 (bottom); Jam4travel: p. 21 (American coins); Christopher David Howells: p. 6; Modellocate: p. 12; Nick Stubbs: p. 8 (right); Wallenrock: p. 13 (middle)
The United States Mint: p. 13 (all except middle)
United States government: p. 19
Other images by Adobe Image Library and Digial Stock

Library and Archives Canada Cataloguing in Publication

Dowdy, Penny
    Money / Penny Dowdy.

(My path to math)
Includes index.
ISBN 978-0-7787-4342-2 (bound).--ISBN 978-0-7787-4360-6 (pbk.)

    1. Counting--Juvenile literature. 2. Money--Juvenile literature.
I. Title. II. Series : Dowdy, Penny. My path to math.

QA113.D69 2008   j513   C2008-906081-4

Library of Congress Cataloging-in-Publication Data

Dowdy, Penny.
    Money / Penny Dowdy.
        p. cm. -- (My path to math)
    Includes index.
    ISBN-13: 978-0-7787-4360-6 (pbk. : alk. paper)
    ISBN-10: 0-7787-4360-8 (pbk. : alk. paper)
    ISBN-13: 978-0-7787-4342-2 (alk. paper)
    ISBN-10: 0-7787-4342-X (alk. paper)
    1. Counting--Juvenile literature. 2. Money--Juvenile literature.
3. Number concept--Juvenile literature. I. Title. II. Series.

    QA113.D69 2008
    513--dc22
                                              2008040150

Crabtree Publishing Company

www.crabtreebooks.com   1-800-387-7650

Published in Canada
Crabtree Publishing
616 Welland Ave.
St. Catharines, Ontario
L2M 5V6

Published in the United States
Crabtree Publishing
PMB16A
350 Fifth Ave., Suite 3308
New York, NY 10118

Published in the United Kingdom
Crabtree Publishing
White Cross Mills
High Town, Lancaster
LA1 4XS

Published in Australia
Crabtree Publishing
386 Mt. Alexander Rd.
Ascot Vale (Melbourne)
VIC 3032

Contents

What is Money?

Money is something that has **value**. **Coins** and **bills** are kinds of money. All around the world, people use money to pay for things.

Many people work for money. They do different kinds of work for different amounts of money. People can buy things with their money.

We use money when
we go shopping.

5

Pennies

Karen walks to the library. That is where her mom works. Karen finds one **penny** and then another.

A penny is a small, round, brown coin. Pennies are worth one **cent** each.

You count pennies by ones.
Four pennies add up to four cents.

Activity Box

You can write four cents like this: 4¢.
What is the sign for cents?

Karen finds pennies on the ground.

Nickels

Karen adds the pennies to the **nickels** in her pocket. A nickel is a thick, round, silver coin. Nickels are worth five cents each. You count nickels by **skip counting** by fives. You count four nickels like this:

5—10—15—20

Four nickels add up to 20 cents.

Activity Box

How can you write 5 cents using the cents sign?

These pictures show both sides
of a nickel from Canada.

Dimes

Karen's mom has flyers that show the hours the library is open. She will pay Karen 10 cents for each flyer Karen hands out. A **dime** is a thin, round, silver coin worth ten cents. You count dimes by skip counting by tens. You count four dimes like this:

10—20—30—40

Four dimes add up to 40 cents.

Activity Box

How many nickels would you need to make 40 cents?

Karen earns money helping her mom at the library.

Quarters

Karen gets paid four quarters.
A **quarter** is a large, round, silver
coin. Quarters are worth 25 cents each.
Skip count them like this:

25—50—75—100

Four quarters are worth 100 cents. Each
quarter is worth 25 pennies. A quarter
equals five nickels. That is the same
amount as two dimes and one nickel.

There are U.S. quarters
for each U.S. state.

One Dollar

Karen stores her quarters at home. She has bills, too. Bills are money made of paper. A bill worth one **dollar** is called a **single**. A dollar is worth 100 cents. Count four dollars like this:

1—2—3—4

You can write 4 dollars like this: $4.

Activity Box

What does the dollar sign look like? You can find a dollar sign on this page!

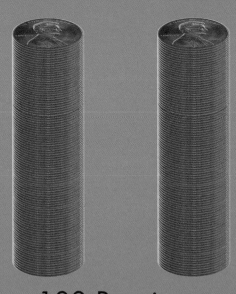   

100 Pennies   20 Nickels   10 Dimes

=

1 Dollar

One dollar is the same as 100
pennies, 20 nickels, or 10 dimes.

Large Bills

Karen even has $5 and $10 bills. Each $5 bill has a 5 on it to show that it is worth $5. Each $10 bill has a 10 on it to show that it is worth $10.

Try counting by tens:

10—20—30—40

Four tens are worth 40 dollars.

Try to skip count these five dollar bills.

Even Larger Bills

A twenty dollar bill is worth twenty $1 bills. Think about four $20 bills. What do four $20 bills add up to?

20—40—60—80

A $50 bill is worth fifty $1 bills. How many ten dollar bills make $50? Five $10 bills are the same as one fifty.

A $100 bill is the same amount as 100 one dollar bills. Would you rather have one $100 bill or 100 one dollar bills?

These bills are worth 80 dollars!

Other Money

Karen lives in a U.S. town close to Canada. She has coins and bills from both countries.

Canada has a $1 coin with a picture of a loon. It is called the **loonie**. Canada has a coin called a **toonie**. It is worth $2.

toonie

Money from different countries looks different.

Glossary

bill Paper money

cent Another word for a penny; ¢

coin A small piece of metal, used as money

dime A small, round, silvery coin worth 10 cents

dollar An amount of money the same as 100 cents; $

equals The same number or amount as

loonie A Canadian $1 coin

nickel A round, silver coin worth 5 cents

penny A small, round, brown coin worth 1 cent

quarter A large, round, silver coin worth 25 cents

skip counting Counting by numbers other than 1

single Another word for a $1 bill

toonie A Canadian $2 coin

value What something is worth

Index

Printed in the U.S.A. — CG